COUNT THEM WITH ME

By **Franicia T. White**

Count Them with Me

by *Franicia Tomokane White*

A WHOLESOME PRESS SOFTCOVER
Copyright © 2016 by Franicia Tomokane White

Wholesome Press
PMB # 24639 PO Box 2428, Pensacola, FL 32513
Website: Wholesome.Press

ISBN: 978-1-943449-18-7
Printed in the United States of America

Illustrations and Book Design by Franicia T. White
Photography by Timothy White
www.timandfranicia.com

This book is a gift for:

_____

_____

_____

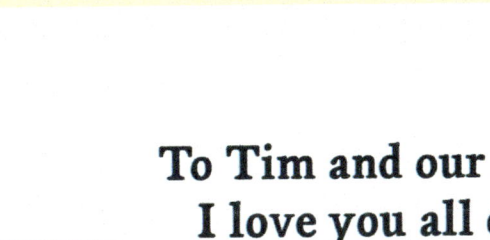

To Tim and our sweet children:
I love you all dearly and am
so thankful to the Lord
for you!

Dear Reader,
I have enjoyed creating this book for you!
May it be a great blessing to you as you learn
your numbers.
❀ Franicia T. White

1 2 3

One, two, three;

One, two, three;

What do I see?

1 2 3

One, two, three;

One, two, three;

Colorful keys.

1 2 3

One, two, three;

One, two, three;

Count them with me.

1 2 3

One, two, three;

One, two, three;

All kinds of trees.

All kinds of apples

And all kinds of cheese;

All kinds of roses

And beautiful leaves!

So many D's

And colorful teas.

1 2 3

One, two, three;

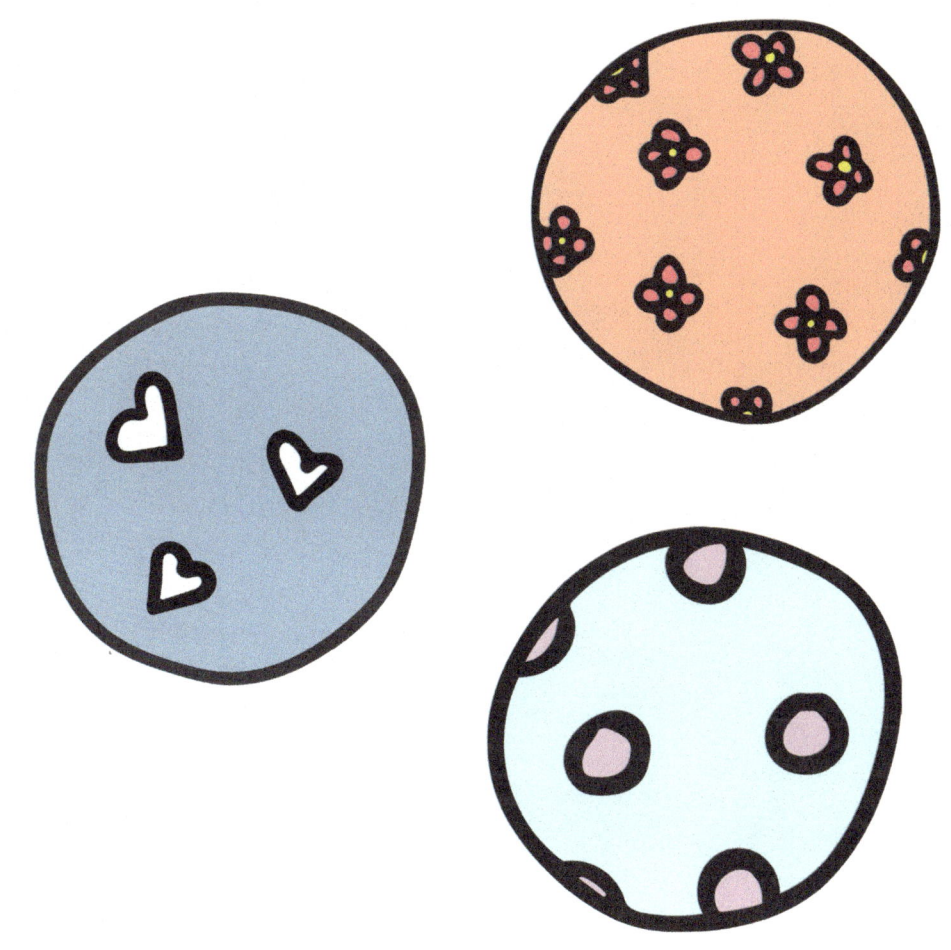

One, two, three;

Count them with me.

0 zero

Numbers

1	one		26	twenty-six
2	two		27	twenty-seven
3	three		28	twenty-eight
4	four		29	twenty-nine
5	five		30	thirty
6	six		31	thirty-one
7	seven		32	thirty-two
8	eight		33	thirty-three
9	nine		34	thirty-four
10	ten		35	thirty-five
11	eleven		36	thirty-six
12	twelve		37	thirty-seven
13	thirteen		38	thirty-eight
14	fourteen		39	thirty-nine
15	fifteen		40	forty
16	sixteen		41	forty-one
17	seventeen		42	forty-two
18	eighteen		43	forty-three
19	nineteen		44	forty-four
20	twenty		45	forty-five
21	twenty-one		46	forty-six
22	twenty-two		47	forty-seven
23	twenty-three		48	forty-eight
24	twenty-four		49	forty-nine
25	twenty-five		50	fifty

Numbers

51	fifty-one		76	seventy-six
52	fifty-two		77	seventy-seven
53	fifty-three		78	seventy-eight
54	fifty-four		79	seventy-nine
55	fifty-five		80	eighty
56	fifty-six		81	eighty-one
57	fifty-seven		82	eighty-two
58	fifty-eight		83	eighty-three
59	fifty-nine		84	eighty-four
60	sixty		85	eighty-five
61	sixty-one		86	eighty-six
62	sixty-two		87	eighty-seven
63	sixty-three		88	eighty-eight
64	sixty-four		89	eighty-nine
65	sixty-five		90	ninety
66	sixty-six		91	ninety-one
67	sixty-seven		92	ninety-two
68	sixty-eight		93	ninety-three
69	sixty-nine		94	ninety-four
70	seventy		95	ninety-five
71	seventy-one		96	ninety-six
72	seventy-two		97	ninety-seven
73	seventy-three		98	ninety-eight
74	seventy-four		99	ninety-nine
75	seventy-five		100	one hundred

1
2
3
4
5
6
7
8
9
10

11
12
13
14
15
16
17
18
19
20

21 🍏🍏🍏🍏🍏🍏🍏🍏🍏🍏 🍏🍏🍏🍏🍏🍏🍏🍏🍏🍏 🍏
22 🍎🍎🍎🍎🍎🍎🍎🍎🍎🍎 🍎🍎🍎🍎🍎🍎🍎🍎🍎🍎 🍎🍎
23 🍏🍏🍏🍏🍏🍏🍏🍏🍏🍏 🍏🍏🍏🍏🍏🍏🍏🍏🍏🍏 🍏🍏🍏
24 🍎🍎🍎🍎🍎🍎🍎🍎🍎🍎 🍎🍎🍎🍎🍎🍎🍎🍎🍎🍎 🍎🍎🍎🍎
25 🍏🍏🍏🍏🍏🍏🍏🍏🍏🍏 🍏🍏🍏🍏🍏🍏🍏🍏🍏🍏 🍏🍏🍏🍏🍏
26 🍎🍎🍎🍎🍎🍎🍎🍎🍎🍎 🍎🍎🍎🍎🍎🍎🍎🍎🍎🍎 🍎🍎🍎🍎🍎🍎
27 🍏🍏🍏🍏🍏🍏🍏🍏🍏🍏 🍏🍏🍏🍏🍏🍏🍏🍏🍏🍏 🍏🍏🍏🍏🍏🍏🍏
28 🍎🍎🍎🍎🍎🍎🍎🍎🍎🍎 🍎🍎🍎🍎🍎🍎🍎🍎🍎🍎 🍎🍎🍎🍎🍎🍎🍎🍎
29 🍏🍏🍏🍏🍏🍏🍏🍏🍏🍏 🍏🍏🍏🍏🍏🍏🍏🍏🍏🍏 🍏🍏🍏🍏🍏🍏🍏🍏🍏
30 🍎🍎🍎🍎🍎🍎🍎🍎🍎🍎 🍎🍎🍎🍎🍎🍎🍎🍎🍎🍎 🍎🍎🍎🍎🍎🍎🍎🍎🍎🍎

31 🍏🍏🍏🍏🍏🍏🍏🍏🍏🍏 🍏🍏🍏🍏🍏🍏🍏🍏🍏🍏 🍏🍏🍏🍏🍏🍏🍏🍏🍏🍏 🍏
32 🍎🍎🍎🍎🍎🍎🍎🍎🍎🍎 🍎🍎🍎🍎🍎🍎🍎🍎🍎🍎 🍎🍎🍎🍎🍎🍎🍎🍎🍎🍎 🍎🍎
33 🍏🍏🍏🍏🍏🍏🍏🍏🍏🍏 🍏🍏🍏🍏🍏🍏🍏🍏🍏🍏 🍏🍏🍏🍏🍏🍏🍏🍏🍏🍏 🍏🍏🍏
34 🍎🍎🍎🍎🍎🍎🍎🍎🍎🍎 🍎🍎🍎🍎🍎🍎🍎🍎🍎🍎 🍎🍎🍎🍎🍎🍎🍎🍎🍎🍎 🍎🍎🍎🍎
35 🍏🍏🍏🍏🍏🍏🍏🍏🍏🍏 🍏🍏🍏🍏🍏🍏🍏🍏🍏🍏 🍏🍏🍏🍏🍏🍏🍏🍏🍏🍏 🍏🍏🍏🍏🍏
36 🍎🍎🍎🍎🍎🍎🍎🍎🍎🍎 🍎🍎🍎🍎🍎🍎🍎🍎🍎🍎 🍎🍎🍎🍎🍎🍎🍎🍎🍎🍎 🍎🍎🍎🍎🍎🍎
37 🍏🍏🍏🍏🍏🍏🍏🍏🍏🍏 🍏🍏🍏🍏🍏🍏🍏🍏🍏🍏 🍏🍏🍏🍏🍏🍏🍏🍏🍏🍏 🍏🍏🍏🍏🍏🍏🍏
38 🍎🍎🍎🍎🍎🍎🍎🍎🍎🍎 🍎🍎🍎🍎🍎🍎🍎🍎🍎🍎 🍎🍎🍎🍎🍎🍎🍎🍎🍎🍎 🍎🍎🍎🍎🍎🍎🍎🍎
39 🍏🍏🍏🍏🍏🍏🍏🍏🍏🍏 🍏🍏🍏🍏🍏🍏🍏🍏🍏🍏 🍏🍏🍏🍏🍏🍏🍏🍏🍏🍏 🍏🍏🍏🍏🍏🍏🍏🍏🍏
40 🍎🍎🍎🍎🍎🍎🍎🍎🍎🍎 🍎🍎🍎🍎🍎🍎🍎🍎🍎🍎 🍎🍎🍎🍎🍎🍎🍎🍎🍎🍎 🍎🍎🍎🍎🍎🍎🍎🍎🍎🍎

41 🍏🍏🍏🍏🍏🍏🍏🍏 🍏🍏🍏🍏🍏🍏🍏🍏 🍏🍏🍏🍏🍏🍏🍏🍏 🍏🍏🍏🍏🍏🍏🍏🍏
🍎

42 🍏🍏🍏🍏🍏🍏🍏🍏 🍏🍏🍏🍏🍏🍏🍏🍏 🍏🍏🍏🍏🍏🍏🍏🍏 🍏🍏🍏🍏🍏🍏🍏🍏
🍎🍎

43 🍏🍏🍏🍏🍏🍏🍏🍏 🍏🍏🍏🍏🍏🍏🍏🍏 🍏🍏🍏🍏🍏🍏🍏🍏 🍏🍏🍏🍏🍏🍏🍏🍏
🍎🍎🍎

44 🍏🍏🍏🍏🍏🍏🍏🍏 🍏🍏🍏🍏🍏🍏🍏🍏 🍏🍏🍏🍏🍏🍏🍏🍏 🍏🍏🍏🍏🍏🍏🍏🍏
🍎🍎🍎🍎

45 🍏🍏🍏🍏🍏🍏🍏🍏 🍏🍏🍏🍏🍏🍏🍏🍏 🍏🍏🍏🍏🍏🍏🍏🍏 🍏🍏🍏🍏🍏🍏🍏🍏
🍎🍎🍎🍎🍎

46 🍏🍏🍏🍏🍏🍏🍏🍏 🍏🍏🍏🍏🍏🍏🍏🍏 🍏🍏🍏🍏🍏🍏🍏🍏 🍏🍏🍏🍏🍏🍏🍏🍏
🍎🍎🍎🍎🍎🍎

47 🍏🍏🍏🍏🍏🍏🍏🍏 🍏🍏🍏🍏🍏🍏🍏🍏 🍏🍏🍏🍏🍏🍏🍏🍏 🍏🍏🍏🍏🍏🍏🍏🍏
🍎🍎🍎🍎🍎🍎🍎

48 🍏🍏🍏🍏🍏🍏🍏🍏 🍏🍏🍏🍏🍏🍏🍏🍏 🍏🍏🍏🍏🍏🍏🍏🍏 🍏🍏🍏🍏🍏🍏🍏🍏
🍎🍎🍎🍎🍎🍎🍎🍎

49 🍏🍏🍏🍏🍏🍏🍏🍏 🍏🍏🍏🍏🍏🍏🍏🍏 🍏🍏🍏🍏🍏🍏🍏🍏 🍏🍏🍏🍏🍏🍏🍏🍏
🍎🍎🍎🍎🍎🍎🍎🍎🍎

50 🍏🍏🍏🍏🍏🍏🍏🍏 🍏🍏🍏🍏🍏🍏🍏🍏 🍏🍏🍏🍏🍏🍏🍏🍏 🍏🍏🍏🍏🍏🍏🍏🍏
🍎🍎🍎🍎🍎🍎🍎🍎🍎🍎

CPSIA information can be obtained
at www.ICGtesting.com
Printed in the USA
BVOW05s0252210417
481740BV00021B/647/P

9 781943 449187